EXPLORE THE WORLD

LIFE SCIENCE

Magnificent Manatees

RUTH MATTISON

TABLE OF CONTENTS

Graceful Swimmers	2
Diet and Habitat	6
Around the World	12
Manatee Babies	14
Dangers for Manatees	16
Glossary/Index	20

PIONEER VALLEY EDUCATIONAL PRESS, INC

GRACEFUL SWIMMERS

Manatees are large **mammals** that swim in the sea. They have large, bulky bodies, but they are very graceful swimmers. Manatees usually move slowly along in the water, but they can swim quite fast for short periods.

Long ago, when sailors first saw manatees with their long tails, they thought the manatees were **MERMAIDS**.

MORE TO EXPLORE

They use their strong flippers and tails to steer themselves, moving their tails up and down to propel their bodies through the water. They can even roll over and do somersaults.

Most manatees are about 10 feet long and weigh about 1,000 pounds.

Manatees are sometimes called "sea cows," but they are more closely related to elephants. Like elephants, manatees have thick, gray, wrinkled skin with very little hair.

Manatees never leave the water. The manatee's nose and **nostrils** are the only parts of its body that you might see above the water's **surface**.

A manatee can stay underwater for up to 20 minutes. After that time, it will surface to breathe air through its nostrils and then go back down. When a manatee swims fast, it uses a lot of energy, so it has to surface for air more often.

MORE TO EXPLORE

Manatees **FLOAT** near the top of the water when resting. This allows them to surface for air while they are sleeping.

DIET AND HABITAT

Manatees can be found in shallow,
slow-moving water.
They like to live near their favorite foods,
sea grass or freshwater plants,
so they don't have to travel far to eat.

Manatees only eat plants.
They eat up to 150 pounds every day.
They use their lips to tear up the plants
and guide the food into their mouths.

Some manatees can live in either freshwater or saltwater, but all manatees drink freshwater. They also can get water from the plants they eat.

As the seasons change and the temperature grows cold, manatees **migrate** to warmer areas.

Long ago, manatees discovered warm water around power plants. Today, thousands of manatees gather in the water near power plants during cold weather.

This is a power plant in Florida. Power plants make electricity and send it to our homes.

Power plants draw cool water from lakes, rivers, and oceans. They use that water to keep their machines from overheating. When the water becomes hot, they pump it back out into the lakes, rivers, or oceans.

This makes the water near power plants a favorite place for manatees to live when the weather gets cold.

Many power plants are closing now. Some people are worried about what the manatees will do after the power plants close and the water cools down.

Before power plants, most manatees that lived near the United States spent the winter by the southern part of Florida.

AROUND THE WORLD

Manatees can be found in lakes, rivers, and oceans along the **coasts** of several countries.

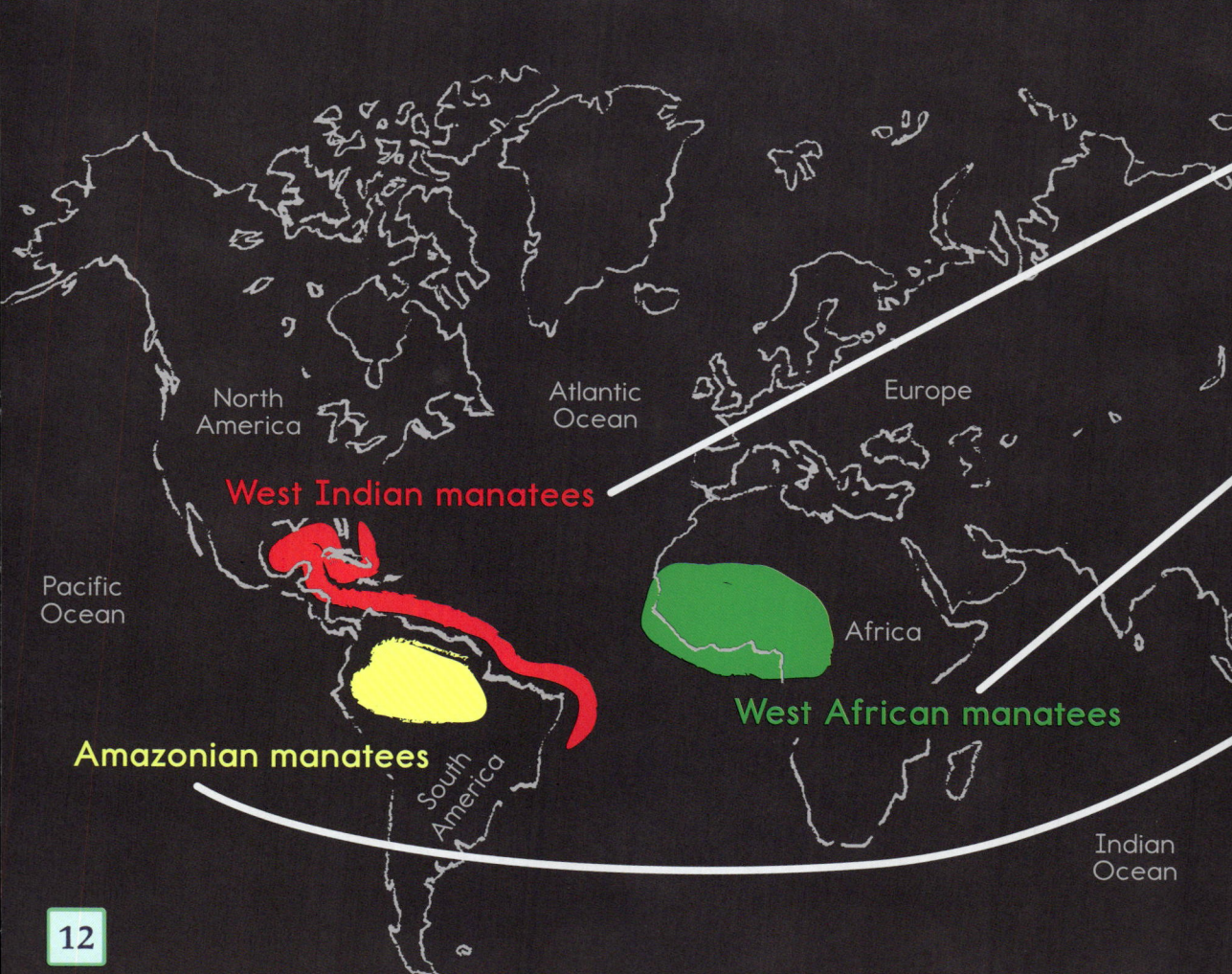

There are three **species** of manatees that live in different parts of the world.

These manatees live off the East Coast of North and South America.

These manatees live in the rivers and waterways along the western coast of Africa.

These manatees are the smallest manatees. They live in the Amazon River in South America.

Australia

MANATEE BABIES

Manatees gather in groups
when it is time to mate.
Manatee babies are born underwater.
The baby is called a calf.
The mother manatee pushes the calf
to the water's surface to take its first breath.
In about one hour, the calf can swim
on its own.

Just like other mammals, a manatee calf drinks its mother's milk. The calf stays with its mother for about two years.

A newborn manatee calf is about 3 to 4 feet long and weighs about 65 pounds.

DANGERS FOR MANATEES

Manatees have no natural enemies. They can live for up to 60 years.

But even though manatees have no natural enemies, they face many dangers.

The greatest threat facing manatees is the power boat. These fast-moving boats are propelled by spinning underwater blades. Crashing into a power boat can kill or seriously injure a manatee, leaving scars down its back and tail.

Manatees also can die from getting tangled in fishing nets and from eating fishhooks.

Other manatees die because of red tide. Red tide is a harmful plant that grows on the sea grasses that manatees eat. Red tide is poisonous to manatees.

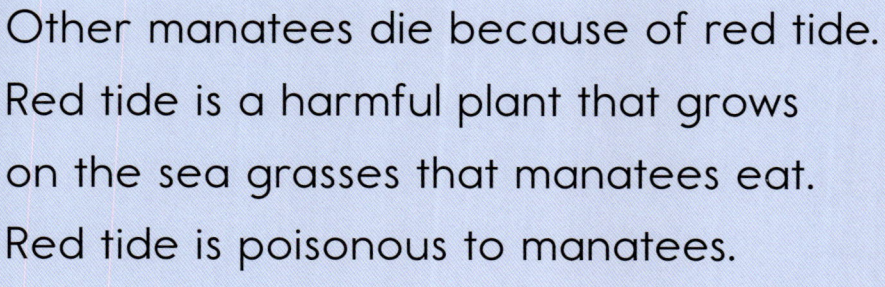

In 1975, Florida's schoolchildren helped name the manatee as the Florida state **marine** mammal.

To make sure that we always have these special animals swimming in our waters, there are laws to protect manatees. It is against the law to injure or harm a manatee. There are also protected areas where manatees can swim, eat, and have babies in safety without being disturbed by people.

Manatees have very small eyes, but they can still see well underwater.

eye

When manatees enter the water, their nostrils shut automatically. This prevents water from entering their lungs.

nostrils

mouth

Manatees are always growing new teeth in the back of their mouths. The new teeth slowly move forward in their mouths as the old teeth in front get worn down.

whiskers

The whiskers on a manatee's snout can sense movement in the water.

PARTS OF A manatee

tail — Manatees move through the water by paddling their tails.

flipper — Manatees use their flippers to turn or spin underwater. Some manatees have fingernails on the ends of their flippers.

GLOSSARY

coasts
areas where the land meets the sea

mammals
animals that feed milk to their young and usually have hair or fur covering most of their skin

marine
plants and animals that live in the sea

migrate
moving from one place to another at different times of the year

nostrils
openings of the nose

species
a group of plants or animals that are all of the same type

surface
the upper layer of land or water

INDEX

Amazonian manatees 12
boats 16
calf 14-15
coasts 12-13
East Coast 13
elephants 4
energy 5
flippers 3
Florida 8, 10, 18
freshwater 6-7
lakes 9, 12
laws 19
mammals 2, 15, 18
marine 18
mermaids 2
migrate 8
North America 12-13
nostrils 5
oceans 9, 12
power plants 8-10
red tide 18
rivers 9, 12, 13
saltwater 7
sea cows 4
sea grass 6, 18
seasons 8
somersaults 3
South America 12-13
species 13
surface 5, 14
swimmers 2
temperature 8
underwater 5, 14, 16
West African manatees 12
West Indian manatees 12
winter 10